0 1 2 3 4 5 6 7 8 9

$2 = 4$ $2 + 4 = 6$ $1 - 1 = 0$

$10 \div 2 = 5$ $22 + 21 = 43$

$68 \div 12 = 5.666$ $5{,}652 \div 700 = 8.074$

$$\frac{x+y}{2} \ge \sqrt{xy}$$

$$\binom{n}{k} = \frac{n!}{(n-k)!\, k!}$$

$$x = \frac{-b \pm \sqrt{b^2 - 4ac}}{2a}$$

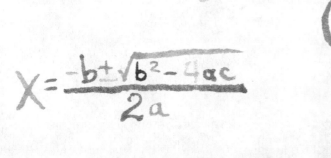

$$A = \sqrt{(s-a)(s-b)(s-c)(s-d)}$$

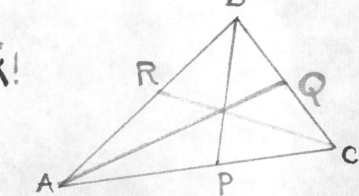

$$\frac{AP}{PC} \cdot \frac{CQ}{BQ} \cdot \frac{BR}{AR} = 1$$

Nothing Stopped Sophie

The Story of Unshakable Mathematician Sophie Germain

Written by **Cheryl Bardoe**

Illustrated by **Barbara McClintock**

LITTLE, BROWN AND COMPANY

NEW YORK   BOSTON

Long ago in Paris, a young girl named Sophie Germain understood that math could do more than measure lengths of silk and tally accounts in her father's shop. In those days, people scoffed at girls for thinking about anything more serious than hair ribbons or what music to play on the pianoforte.

But nothing stopped Sophie.

Telling Sophie not to think about math was like telling a bird not to soar.

Ideas came to Sophie day and night, and she sneaked out of bed
to study math while others slept. Monsieur and Madame Germain
worried that being smart would bring their daughter heartbreak
and scorn.

So they seized Sophie's candles...

they stopped lighting fires in her room...

and they snatched away her warm dresses,

desperate to make her stay tucked into bed.

Still, nothing stopped Sophie.

One morning Sophie was found bundled in blankets, asleep at her desk, next to a pot of ink that had frozen solid. Finally, Sophie's parents let their daughter indulge her mathematical dreams. For a girl to become a mathematician would be impossible anyway.

Sophie grew up during the French Revolution, when starving peasants rioted against rich kings and nobles who feasted on sausages, salads, and sweets. When the streets were unsafe outdoors, Sophie's parents kept her indoors. As cries for equality echoed from the roof tiles, she cherished how math could make sense of the world.

Math,
    with its clear and simple laws.
Math,
    with its strong sense of order.
Math,
    which defines when the world is in balance.

Curled up in her father's library, Sophie barely heard the distant cannons that rattled the shutters.

Sophie discovered that mathematicians use numbers as poets use letters—as a language to question, explore, and solve the secrets of the universe. She read how ancient Greeks wrote equations that made the impossible possible:

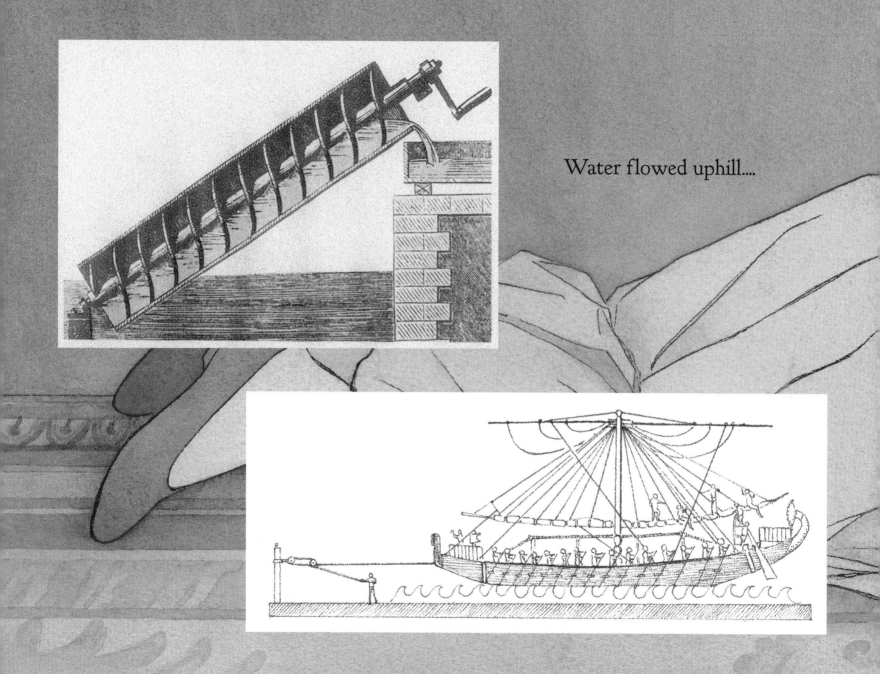

Water flowed uphill....

A lone man pulled mighty ships ashore....

A scholar measured the size of the earth....

Sophie longed to become a mathematician and write such poems of her own.

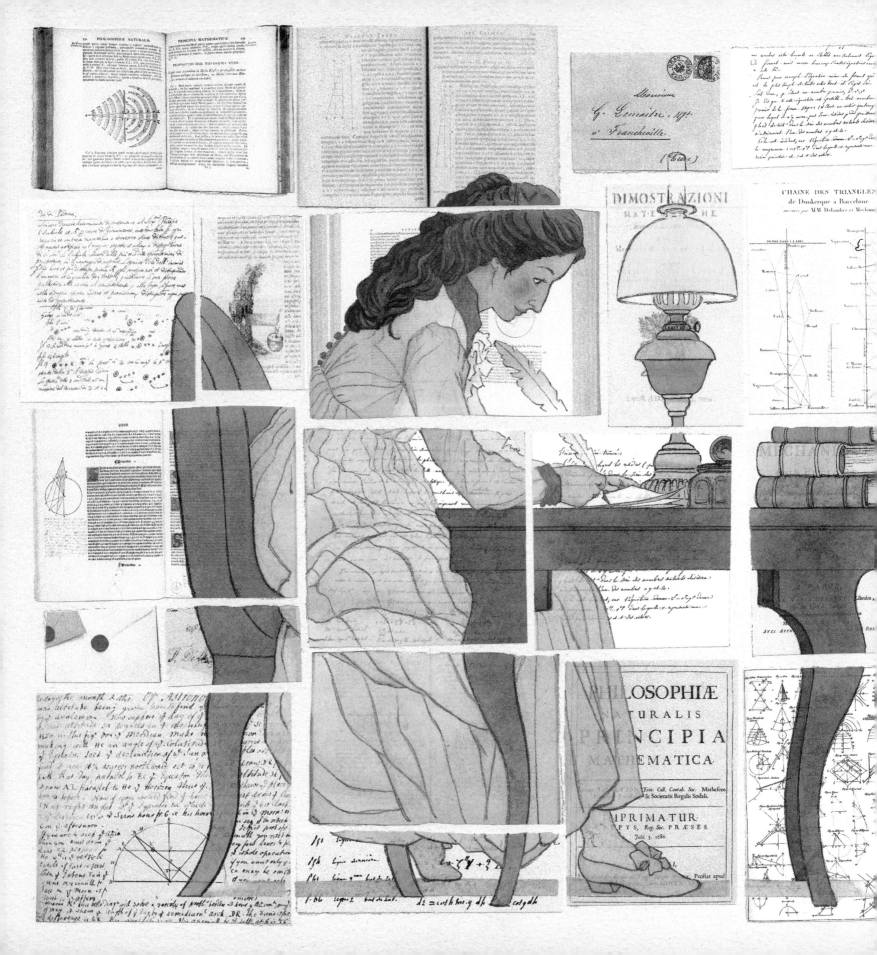

By the time Sophie was nineteen, the French Revolution had simmered down, and it was safe to walk the streets of Paris again. Sophie wanted to attend a university, but no professor would read a woman's work. So she secretly acquired notes from math classes and sent in homework by mail. She signed her papers "Monsieur LeBlanc."

Then one day, a knock came at the door....

Professor Joseph-Louis Lagrange had come to meet the mysterious student who sent in extraordinary homework without coming to class.

We'll never know who received the greater shock: Professor Lagrange could not have guessed that Monsieur LeBlanc was a modest young lady in a ruffled blouse with dark hair in a topknot. And Sophie could not have imagined a visit from a world-famous scholar.

Was her dream about to take flight?

With Sophie's secret discovered, news of the girl prodigy rippled through Paris. Gossips couldn't imagine a girl so smart until they met her themselves, and soon Sophie's calendar swelled with dinner parties.

She hardly knew what to say in these stuffy drawing rooms, surrounded by gawkers in finery. She ached to talk seriously about math, yet no mathematician would take a young lady truly under his wing.

Still, nothing stopped Sophie.

She kept up her studies. She seized every chance to chat with scholars at luncheons and in salons. Under her pen name, she wrote to one of the most brilliant mathematicians ever. Carl Friedrich Gauss even wrote back—but his letters stopped coming soon after he discovered that Mr. LeBlanc was a woman.

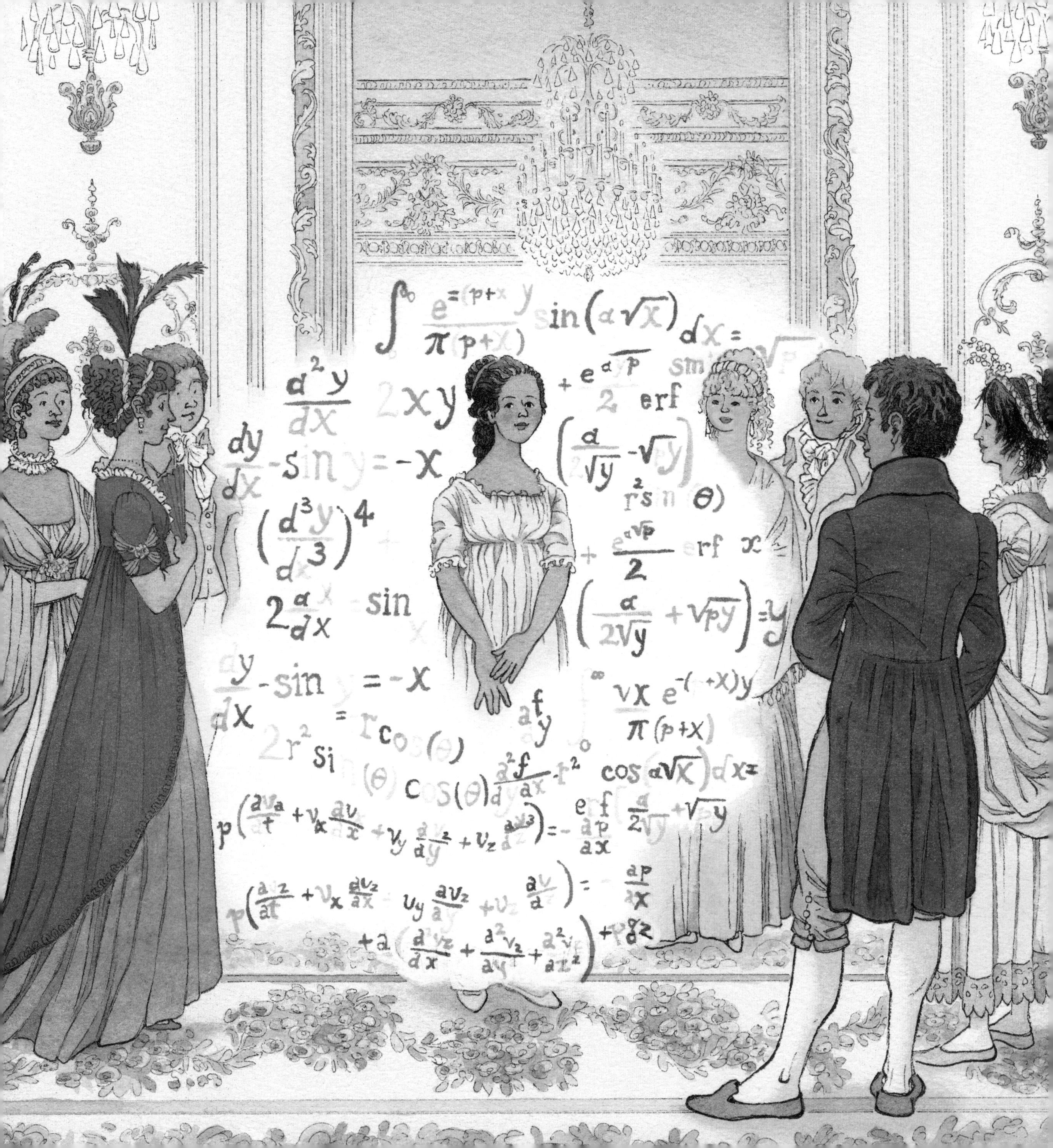

At age thirty-two, Sophie witnessed an experiment that revealed the hidden laws of math at work in our everyday world. She saw a scientist sprinkle sand onto a glass plate. As he rubbed a violin bow against the plate's edge, vibrations shook the glass until it rang out with sound. Astonished, Sophie watched the sand dance across the plate! It formed circles...then diamonds...then figure eights.

The higher the note, the more quickly the vibrations shook the plate, and the more intricate the sand's pattern became.

Suddenly, Sophie realized that every hand knocking on a door...her own boots clicking along the cobblestones...every motion sent vibrations surging through nearby objects, just as waves flowed through water.

The rest of Paris was agog, too. The prestigious Academy of Sciences offered a medal worth 3,000 francs to anyone who could find a mathematical formula that would predict patterns of vibration. This information could affect buildings, bridges, and who knew what else? How much vibration was too much? At what point would an object break?

Academy scholars called the problem impossible. Their heads spun just thinking about the many ways vibration might move an object.

But nothing stopped Sophie.

Just as math measures how bird wings move up and down during flight, Sophie knew math could measure a surface moving up and down from vibration. She made her best guesses at what would affect this movement. Then she added and subtracted and multiplied and divided. Sophie spent two years trying numbers in different combinations to write her equations. Then she submitted her work to the academy. And this time...Sophie used her own name.

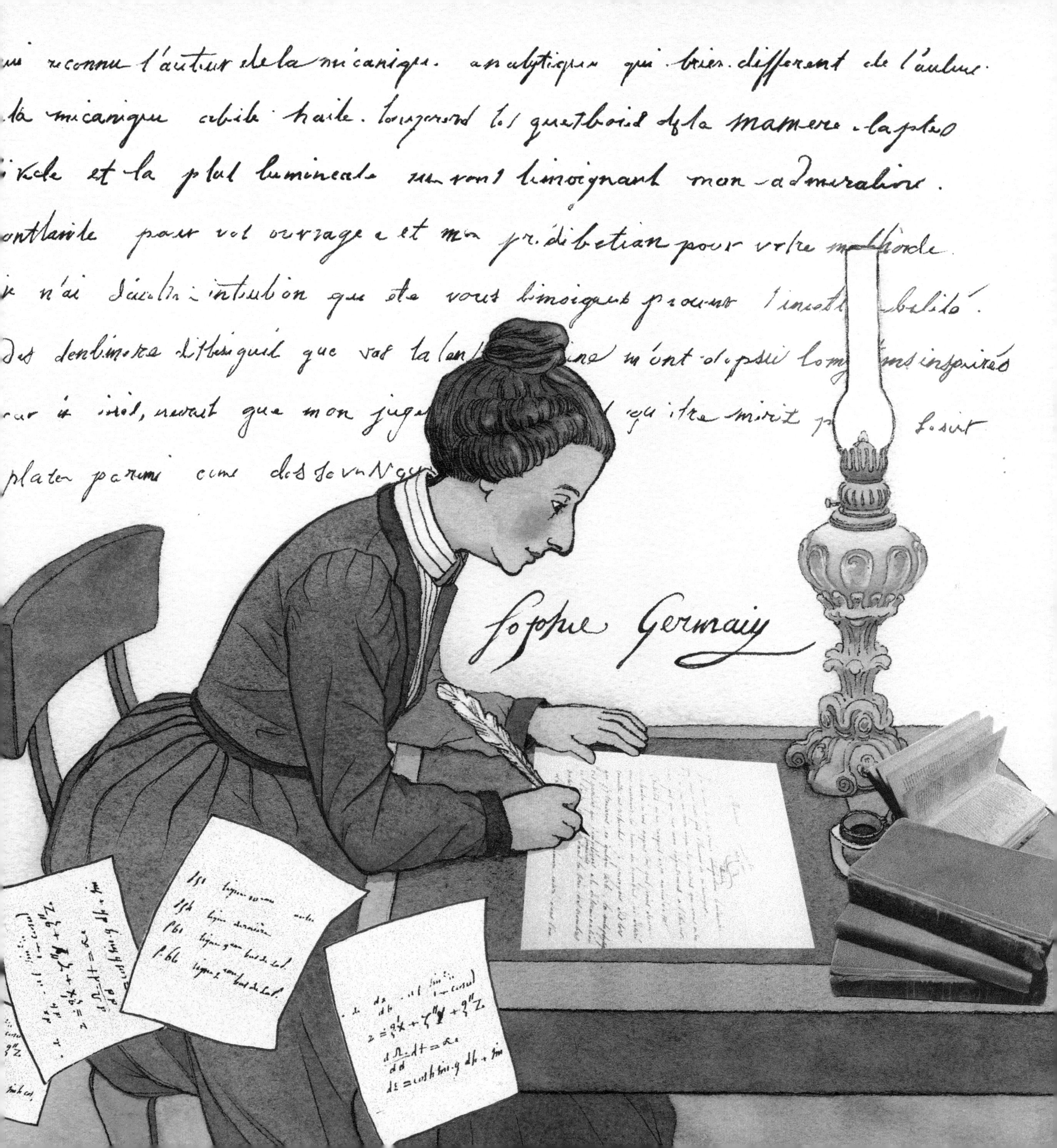
Sophie Germain

Sophie's work sent shock waves through Paris. The contest had received only one entry—and it had come from a woman!

Yet Sophie's solution was incorrect. When the academy extended the contest, Sophie returned to work. For two more years she tested her predictions by vibrating sand on plates.

Finally, after thousands of calculations, the sand moved just how Sophie's numbers foretold. Her equation was as precise and eloquent as a poem.

Sophie submitted the only entry to the academy again. This time scholars agreed that her equation was correct! But they rejected her explanation for *why* it worked.

Still, nothing stopped Sophie. She revised her research and submitted it to the academy one more time....

In 1816, Sophie Germain became the first woman to win a grand prize from the Royal Academy of Sciences. After six years, she had shaken the academy enough to shatter its resistance. No one could deny that she was a mathematician now.

"The human spirit," she later reflected, "requires more resources inside when outside it has less."

After Sophie's work, mathematicians sought even better ways to predict vibration patterns. Eventually their discoveries made it possible to build the Eiffel Tower in Paris and modern skyscrapers and lengthy bridges all over the world.

Sophie is celebrated today because nothing stopped her. Her fearlessness and perseverance have inspired many people.

Perhaps she will also inspire you.

MORE ABOUT SOPHIE

The French Revolution was a turbulent time to be a teenager. The middle and lower classes of French society no longer trusted rich nobles and royal families to look out for them, and they wanted a say in governing themselves. Rage at high taxes and widespread famine ran so high that no one was truly safe. Sometimes people were beaten in the streets just for not wearing the red, white, and blue that was the symbol of revolution.

The king and queen resisted change until their own subjects executed them in 1793. By the time Sophie was nineteen, she had lived under at least four different kinds of governments, and thousands of people had lost their heads at the guillotine for angering one side or another. Amid this bloodshed was exciting talk of equality and liberty. Yet women did not receive the right to vote as citizens in any of the new governments that evolved.

Most girls in Sophie's time did not go to school and were lucky if they received an education at home. Indeed, any woman who expressed herself as an intellectual risked becoming the target of gossip and ridicule, although expectations were slowly changing. When Sophie's mathematical talents became known, her gentleness and modest manners saved her from becoming a social outcast. Sophie never married and devoted her life to math.

In addition to her work on vibration, Sophie is one of the few people to have made progress on another "impossible" problem. Around 1630, a mathematician named Pierre de Fermat stated that a specific kind of equation would not work for any number other than 1 or 2. But he had no proof. Sophie was the first mathematician to prove his theory correct for a large group of numbers, which ever since have been called Sophie Germain prime numbers. Sophie's notebooks show that she hoped one day to solve the entire puzzle! Perhaps she would have succeeded if she had not died from breast cancer at age fifty-five. The puzzle, called Fermat's Last Theorem, was finally proven in 1994.

IS THIS MATH OR SCIENCE?

Science and math are deeply connected. The sand that Sophie watched dancing across the glass plate was bouncing off the places that moved the most and resting in the places that stayed almost still. We often study vibration and sound waves as parts of physics, which is the science of how things move. Yet without numbers to measure, describe, and define relationships, our understanding of physics would not be very useful.

We know, for example, that threading a rope over a wheel to form a pulley makes it easier to move heavy objects. Without math, however, the Greek mathematician Archimedes would not have known how many pulley wheels and what length of rope were needed for a single person to pull a boat ashore. With math, we can use an equation to figure out how much extra force a pulley adds when we pull on the rope. In the same way, Sophie's equation described the relationship between the factors that influenced the vibrations.

If you'd like to know more about the equations discovered by the ancient Greeks, some of which are illustrated in this book's art, look up "Archimedes screw," "Archimedes pulley system," and "Eratosthenes pillars and shadows."

DISCOVER THE EFFECTS OF VIBRATION FOR YOURSELF!

Run a wet finger around the rim of a thin wineglass. If you rub hard and long enough, the glass will resonate with sound. Even though the glass doesn't appear to move, the sound comes from vibration caused by your finger rubbing the glass. Would the glass vibrate differently if it were a different thickness? Or a different shape? Sophie explored these and other questions to find her equation for how vibrations work.

You can see re-creations of the same experiment that captured Sophie's attention by searching the Internet for "vibration," "salt," and "Chladni," which is the name of the scientist who performed the experiments in Sophie's time. Although we understand it better now, seeing the sand (or salt) dance is just as amazing as it was more than 200 years ago.

SELECTED BIBLIOGRAPHY

Bucciarelli, L. L. and Dworsky, N. *Sophie Germain*. New York: Springer Dordrecht, 1980.

Stupuy, H., ed. *Oeuvres Philosophiques de Sophie Germain Suivies de Pensees et de Lettres Inedites*. Elibron Classics series ed. Paris, France: Paul Ritti, 1879.

Anderson, James M. *Daily Life During the French Revolution*. New York: Greenwood, 2007.

A NOTE FROM CHERYL BARDOE

When I first heard about Sophie Germain, I was immediately impressed. I love how she sought order amid chaos, how she boldly pursued math, and how she never gave up.

Writing about a historical subject, even with stacks of research, forces an author to make interesting choices. Many details from Sophie's personal life—such as her first meeting with Professor Lagrange—are not precisely recorded. Some sources suggest that Lagrange discovered the true identity of Mr. LeBlanc when he arrived at Sophie's address. Others imply he discovered her identity *before* coming to call. All agree that the two met and that Mr. LeBlanc turning out to be a woman caused a stir. Still other details are perfectly recorded, yet would add unnecessary complication to the story. Due to shifting political winds, the Royal Academy of Sciences changed its name several times during Sophie's lifetime. Yet this group of scholars remained largely stable in its membership and purpose, so highlighting the name changes would distract from Sophie's story.

Even when sources and historians agree on facts, their significance is subject to interpretation. Sophie's correspondence illustrates that some scholars took a kindly interest in her work. Yet even her strongest supporters treated her differently from promising mathematicians who were men. Thus, from a modern lens, we recognize the obstacles Sophie faced, even though she received what in her day would have been considered "extra" opportunities for a woman.

Wouldn't it be wonderful if history always recorded the actions, ideas, and feelings of those who intrigue us? This book relies on Sophie's correspondence, a biography written by a close friend after her death, her journals, and writings by historians of her life and times. Even with an imperfect record, enough information exists to reveal an incredible person and story.

I am deeply grateful for the vision that illustrator Barbara McClintock brought to this book. I am thankful for editor Deirdre Jones, who did not shy away from exploring historical dilemmas or celebrating mathematical complexities. And I am eternally appreciative of my husband, Dr. Matthew Bardoe, who inspires young people to love math every day. Math is a field that sometimes intimidates—yet when it is embraced, we see its power everywhere in our world.

A NOTE FROM BARBARA MCCLINTOCK

When I was approached to illustrate *Nothing Stopped Sophie*, I was terrified. I was an abysmal math student, and the thought of illustrating a book about a brilliant mathematician was ironic at best. Once I became involved in the work, though, I noticed parallels between Sophie and myself, and found ways to approach the project that married the mathematical with the artistic.

The first step was to take a nonliteral visual approach to the story. The manuscript inspired me to use colorful markers, gouache, and collage—techniques new to me, and thrilling to explore. I wanted to reference Sophie's work on patterns of vibration and to echo Cheryl Bardoe's allusions to vibration and motion in the text. I envisioned numbers swirling around Sophie, bright and joyful, but also cocooning her from gawking gossips at a party and rising up in the streets of Paris to illustrate the violence of her childhood. It was during the French Revolution that Sophie became fascinated with the work of Archimedes, teaching herself calculus, Greek, and Latin, and here I found a link between us: I am self-taught as an artist. (I've also felt the awkwardness of being at a party with no one I could talk to about my work.)

Taking a nonliteral approach also allowed me to illustrate certain moments—such as Sophie winning the academy's prize—in a conceptual way. My research revealed that she didn't receive the award in person; in fact, women were only allowed into the academy building accompanied by their mathematician and scientist husbands. Sophie's winning formula flows out of her pen around the all-male members of the academy, their top hats and coattails flying in the gale of numbers. Similarly, in the scene where Sophie witnesses the experiment with sand, initially I'd drawn loops of figure eights and simple diamonds. But then a friend sent me helpful videos and photos of Chladni plate patterns, and I ended up incorporating these more accurate shapes into the illustration. I also played with the vibration motif in the image of the newspaper boy yelling out the headline, his shouts bending buildings and sending a cloud of birds tumbling through the air and on to the next double-page spread, reinforcing the story's imagery of birds and flight.

My profound thanks go to my editor Deirdre Jones, art director Saho Fujii, author Cheryl Bardoe, and the Little, Brown Books for Young Readers team for trusting this abysmal math student with a text that challenged me to experiment artistically and to never give up—just like Sophie.

To my dad, who also likes to ponder puzzles —CB ✛ To David Johnson, my second set of eyes —BM

ABOUT THIS BOOK

This book was edited by Deirdre Jones and designed by Jamie W. Yee, with art direction by Saho Fujii. The production was supervised by Erika Schwartz, and the production editor was Annie McDonnell. The text was set in Kennerly, and the display type is Baskerville.

Text copyright © 2018 by Cheryl Bardoe • Illustrations copyright © 2018 by Barbara McClintock • Cover illustration copyright © 2018 by Barbara McClintock • Cover design by Jamie W. Yee • Cover copyright © 2018 by Hachette Book Group, Inc. • Hachette Book Group supports the right to free expression and the value of copyright. The purpose of copyright is to encourage writers and artists to produce the creative works that enrich our culture. • The scanning, uploading, and distribution of this book without permission is a theft of the author's intellectual property. If you would like permission to use material from the book (other than for review purposes), please contact permissions@hbgusa.com. Thank you for your support of the author's rights. • Little, Brown and Company • Hachette Book Group • 1290 Avenue of the Americas, New York, NY 10104 • Visit us at LBYR.com • First Edition: June 2018 • Little, Brown and Company is a division of Hachette Book Group, Inc. The Little, Brown name and logo are trademarks of Hachette Book Group, Inc. • The publisher is not responsible for websites (or their content) that are not owned by the publisher. • Library of Congress Cataloging-in-Publication Data • Names: Bardoe, Cheryl, 1971– | McClintock, Barbara, illustrator. • Title: Nothing Stopped Sophie : a story of unshakable mathematician sophie germain / written by Cheryl Bardoe ; illustrated by Barbara McClintock. • Description: New York : Little, Brown and Company, [2018] • Audience: Age 4-8. • Identifiers: LCCN 2016040477| ISBN 9780316278201 (hardcover) | ISBN 9780316394284 (library edition ebook) | ISBN 9780316394291 (ebook) • Subjects: LCSH: Germain, Sophie, 1776-1831. | Women Mathematicians–France–Biography–Juvenile literature. | Mathematicians–France–Biography–Juvenile literature. | Mathematics–France–History–19th century–Juvenile literature. • Classification: LCC QA29.G468 B37 2018 | DDC 510.92 [B]–dc23 • LC record available at https://lccn.loc.gov/2016040477 • ISBNs: 978-0-316-27820-1 (hardcover), 978-0-316-39429-1 (ebook), 978-0-316-41149-3 (ebook), 978-0-316-41150-9 (ebook) • PRINTED IN CHINA • APS • 10 9 8 7 6 • Pages 2, 3, 38, and 39: Vintage paper backdrop © Andrius_Saz/Shutterstock.com • page 4: Watercolor texture © white snow/Shutterstock.com • page 4: Hand-drawn letters © cosmaa/Shutterstock.com

$$\iint \left(\frac{\partial u}{\partial x} + \frac{\partial v}{\partial y}\right) dx\,dy$$

$$\int_2^3 \int_0^3 \int 8xyz\,dz\,dx\,dy = 15 \qquad \begin{bmatrix} \dfrac{d^2 f}{dx^2} & \dfrac{d^2 f}{dx\,dy} \\[2mm] \dfrac{d^2 f}{dx\,dy} & \dfrac{d^2 f}{dy^2} \end{bmatrix}$$

$$\lim_{x \to \infty} \frac{\pi(x)}{\frac{x}{\ln(x)}} = 1$$

$$\int_0^\infty \frac{e^{(p-x)y}}{\pi(p+x)} \sin(a\sqrt{x})\,dx = \sinh(x\sqrt{p})\left(2\sqrt{y}\,\sqrt{py}\right) r$$

$$\frac{dy}{dx} - \sin y = -x \qquad 2r^2 \sin(\theta)\cos(\theta) \qquad \frac{\partial^2 f}{\partial y \partial}$$

$$= -\operatorname{erf}\left[\frac{\partial}{2\sqrt{y}} + \sqrt{py}\right] \quad \left(\frac{\partial v_z}{\partial t} + v_x \frac{\partial v^2}{\partial x} + v_y \frac{\partial v_z}{\partial y} + v_z \frac{\partial v}{\partial z}\right)$$

$$\frac{4(x^p - 1)}{x - 1} = y^2 \pm pz^2 \qquad x^4 + 4y^4 = \left((x+y)^2 + y^2\right)\left((x-y)^2 + y^2\right) = \left(x^2\right.$$